Original title:
Life's Like a Bag of Chips—Unexpected and Crunchy

Copyright © 2025 Creative Arts Management OÜ
All rights reserved.

Author: Henry Beaumont
ISBN HARDBACK: 978-1-80566-177-1
ISBN PAPERBACK: 978-1-80566-472-7

A Journey in Every Bite

Each crunch brings a surprise,
A flavor burst that defies.
Some sweet, some quite sour,
Every bite holds power.

From barbecue to sour cream,
Every chip's like a dream.
A rollercoaster of taste,
No moment ever goes to waste.

Bits of Bliss and Bitterness

A chip can be a delight,
Then turn on you overnight.
With every crunch, a twist,
You'll laugh then shake your fist.

Salted joy meets spicy fright,
Each handful's a new insight.
Crunchy moments to explore,
What's behind that crispy door?

Crumbs of Curiosity

Tiny crumbs tell a tale,
Of savory, sweet, or stale.
Take a chance, don't be shy,
Next bite could make you cry!

Finding a chip with a twist,
Oh, how could this be missed?
Your taste buds dance and sing,
Like they're prancing in spring.

Unexpected Flavors on the Path

Flavors pop with every crunch,
A daring dip or a punch.
Each bag a treasure chest,
Some flavors simply the best.

You think you've seen it all,
Then a new crunch makes you sprawl.
Mystery in each bite,
Savor the snack, take flight!

Explorations in Every Crisp

Never know what's inside,
Each crunch a bold surprise.
Sea salt or a hint of cheese,
Makes tasting out a tease.

In every crinkle, fun awaits,
A treasure hunt on plates.
Some flavors zing, others melt,
Joy in every bite you've felt.

Surprising Layers

Layers stacked with glee,
Cheddar, barbecue, oh me!
What's hiding at the bottom there?
A spicy kick—beware, beware!

Each bag tells a tale,
You've picked the holy grail.
Beneath the top, a crowded crew,
A symphony of tastes for you.

Moments of Munching Mystery

Crinkle, crunch—what's this treat?
A puzzle that's quite neat.
Sweet and savory embrace,
A waltz of flavors in the race.

Grab a handful, take a chance,
Each bite brings a silly dance.
Lime or maybe dill surprise,
Who knew snacking can be wise?

The Journey of Texture

From crisp to smooth and back again,
A journey through the snack den.
Each texture tells a tale of delight,
In every crunch, pure appetite.

With flavors that twist and twirl,
Unexpected joy begins to unfurl.
So grab a bag, let's explore,
The world of chips has much in store!

Curiosity in Every Bite

Open the pack, hear that snap,
A mystery awaits in every flap.
With flavors wild, the fun runs high,
You never know who'll make you sigh.

A hint of lime, a dash of spice,
Beneath the crunch, oh, isn't it nice?
Each bite a riddle, a tasty quest,
You laugh and munch, it's simply the best.

Adventure in Crisps

In a bowl, they mingle and wait,
Each chip a journey, oh, what fate!
Ranch or barbecue, what to choose?
With every crunch, there's so much to lose.

Grab a few, toss them with flair,
Who knew adventure was hiding in there?
Every chip tells a tale so grand,
Together we treasure the taste we planned.

Flavors of the Unexpected

Open the bag, prepared for more,
Sweet or savory, who's keeping score?
From sea salt highs to dill pickle lows,
Each chip a surprise, as the laughter grows.

With a zesty twang or a gentle kiss,
It's a flavor rollercoaster, you can't miss.
Reach in deep, take a wild chance,
You might just find a chipsy romance.

Crunchy Tales Await

Gather round, let's share our snacks,
Each crunch a story, no need to relax.
In cheesy shades or spicy reds,
We crunch on laughter, hearts and heads.

A munch together, oh, what a treat,
With friends beside, the pack's never complete.
Each flavor whispers, come take a ride,
In every bite, let joy be your guide.

Experiencing the Expectation

You grab a bag with hope in mind,
Each crisp a treasure, what will you find?
A salty hit or a zesty flare,
You dig right in, with flavors to share.

But oh, what's this? A seaweed hue,
Not on the list, but better than stew!
With every crunch comes laughter's thrill,
Like dodging raindrops, or climbing a hill.

The Unpredictable Flavor Trail

In every crunch, a tale unfolds,
Some bites are bold, and some are cold.
You think you're safe with the classic chip,
But here comes barbecue—your taste buds flip.

A pop of vinegar, oh so bright,
Followed by cheddar—what a delight!
Each handful brims with whimsical flair,
Life's bag of crunches is never too rare.

Crumbs of Surprise

A whiff of cheese, but what is this?
A chip so spicy, it's hard to miss!
With crunchy bits crumbling down your shirt,
You wear the snacks like a badge of dirt.

An onion ring, when least expected,
Dancing with flavors, so well connected.
As laughter bubbles up like a spritz,
These crumbs of surprise are hit or miss!

Flavor Fluctuations

One minute sweet, the next is heat,
A taste explosion is hard to beat!
Like a movie twist that makes you grin,
Each chip is a gamble where no one can win.

A sour burst'll catch you off guard,
It's like a joke told when life gets hard.
When munching along this crunchy spree,
Every flavor is wild and always free!

Unknown Tastes Await

A potato in a cloak, oh so sly,
You take a bite, and wonder why.
Sweet and salty, what's next in line?
Oh, the thrill of flavor, how divine!

One chip's a mystery, the next a jest,
Could this be pickle? Or maybe zest?
On this adventure, who'll take the lead?
Grab a handful, it's all you need!

Notes of Flavor Adventure

Barbecue whispers, a cheesy grin,
Sour cream giggles, where do we begin?
With each crunchy morsel, a twist unfolds,
A symphony of tastes, bright and bold.

What's that—a hint of something strange?
A spicy surprise, or a flavor exchange?
Each bag a journey, we chew with glee,
Tasting the odd, come journey with me!

Graphs of Crunchy Surprises

If chips had a chart, what a sight to see,
Lines of delicious, in harmony.
A scatterplot of snacks, crunchy delight,
Each crunch a data point, oh what a night!

Potato pie, or dill pickle kiss,
What's trending today? We can't miss this!
We're mapping our munchies, with laughter we share,
In the crispy wilderness, we've no time to spare!

The Flavor Parade

Marching through taste, in a potato brigade,
Dancing with spices, their bright charade.
Salsa drums beating, a piquant array,
Join the fun, it's the flavor parade!

Onion rings marching, a crunchy salute,
Chili chips prancing, oh what a hoot!
Popcorn confetti, a crunchy array,
In this joyous festival, we'll always stay!

Ripples of Flavor

In the snack aisle, choices abound,
Popping open, a new joy's found.
Sour or spicy, each bite a thrill,
One might taste like a pickle hill.

Lurking flavors hide and sneak,
A surprise burst—who knew they'd peek?
Sweet with a touch of chili's lust,
Into the unknown, we dive and trust.

A Symphony of Crunch

Crisp crescendos in each little bag,
Every munch is a crunchy snag.
Some fall silent, others sing loud,
Each handful's a whimsical crowd.

Twirling flavors dance on the tongue,
Popping surprises, oh how they've sprung!
The zest of lemon, the heat of the fire,
A crunchy concert we all admire.

Pantries of Possibility

In pantries packed with secret delight,
Each snack whispers, 'Come take a bite!'
From cheesy dreams to spicy thrills,
There's hidden treasure that always fills.

Choices await like a game of chance,
Grab a handful, and start your dance.
Some chips are angels, others like devils,
Mixing sweet spices like clever rebels.

Echoes of the Unexpected

Who knew this crisp would pop so right?
The flavor echoes, a joyous flight.
Beneath the surface, surprises hide,
A crunchy tale that's hard to bide.

With each rustle, a giggle ensues,
The pranks of flavor gently amuse.
Let's celebrate snacks that dare to grin,
In this playful bag, let the fun begin!

Taste Bud Tango

In the cupboard, a bag does hide,
Crackling whispers, come take a ride.
Flavors dance with a joyful cheer,
Each bite a surprise, oh so dear.

Sour cream dreams and barbecue flair,
Cheddar clouds float in the air.
Crunching joy, a festive sound,
In every chip, delight is found.

Crisps of Chance

A bag pops open, excitement alive,
Guess the flavor? We'll take a dive!
Spicy turns sweet, oh what a twist,
Each crispy bite, too fun to miss.

Potato humor in every crunch,
Laughter erupts with every munch.
The gamble of taste, a playful bet,
With each new chip, more fun is met.

The Crunch that Delights

Golden treasures stacked high and bold,
Each crisp tells stories, deliciously told.
A munch for the ages, a thin, bright slice,
Unexpected flavors that tease and entice.

From tangy to sweet, a wild parade,
Craving the crunch, we happily wade.
Nothing compares to this cheerful bite,
Joy-packed parcels that feel just right.

Savoring the Little Things

Tiny moments, like chips in a bowl,
Each one carries a happy soul.
Taste of adventure in every pack,
Unexpected pleasures keep calling back.

The laughter shared with a crunch or two,
Simple delights that make us woo.
In salty bites, the world feels bright,
Let's celebrate these crispy delights!

Morsels of Joy and Regret

In a world of salty bites,
We gather up our cheer,
Each crunch reveals a twist,
And perhaps a hint of fear.

Some snacks are sweet, some plain,
We munch with glee, then sigh,
Life's flavors shift and change,
Like crumbs that drift and fly.

The Crinkle of Fortune

A rustle in the bag, we peek,
What treasure will we find?
Will it be spicy joy or mild?
The thrill is one of a kind.

Each bite a chance encounter,
A gamble in disguise,
With every crunch we wonder,
What new surprise lies inside?

Flavorful Chaos in a Crunch

The chips all tumble, a wild dance,
Spicy, cheesy joy,
Each flavor tells a story,
Of fun, and mess, and ploy.

We laugh at every crumble,
As we try to keep it neat,
But the chaos is contagious,
And the munching is a treat!

Crispy Moments

In the crunch of crispy layers,
We find our silly fate,
Each morsel brings a chuckle,
Then we can't help but wait.

For flavors keep on popping,
With each surprising chip,
Moments crispy, fun and fleeting,
As we savor every sip.

Messy Living

With crumbs upon our clothes,
We embrace the sweet disaster,
In the mess of living boldly,
We discover joy, much faster.

Each crunch speaks of adventure,
In flavors rich and bright,
So let's dive in together,
And share this tasty bite!

Salty Surprises

In a world of flavors, we take a bite,
Each crunch revealing a twist in the night.
Some chips are spicy, some sweetly bland,
Keep munching along, it's weird but grand.

A picnic with pals, there's laughter and cheers,
One chip goes flying—oh dear, not my peers!
The crunch of a secret, the rustle of fate,
Grab another handful, it's never too late.

Crunching Through Chaos

Life is a party with snacks on the floor,
Each flavor a reason to laugh and explore.
A nibble of joy, a sprinkle of sass,
With crumbs on our face, we'll get through this class.

Dancing with chips while the world spins around,
Each crunch tells a story, every sound profound.
From sour to sweet, the mix makes you grin,
So let's snack on the chaos, and dig right in!

Hidden Flavors of Existence

In the depths of the bag, surprises await,
Crisps of delight that are worth the debate.
A hint of a mystery, a dash of weird cheer,
Each chip a reminder that fun's always near.

Some flavors are bold, while others are shy,
Like friends on this journey, oh my, oh my!
From tiny to large, they all have a role,
Together they make up the flavor of soul.

The Crunch of Everyday Moments

Beneath the surface, the crunching begins,
Each snap a reminder of how silly life spins.
With laughter as spice and joy as the base,
Every chew brings out a smile on our face.

From the mundane tasks to the wildest ride,
Every chip on our plate is something applied.
So let's pop and crackle through thick and through thin,
In the bag of existence, let's dive right in!

The Crunch Beneath

In the cupboard, a surprise,
Potato dreams in disguise.
When the bag unseals with flair,
Popcorn wishes in the air.

Each crisp a story to tell,
Some are spicy, some as well.
With a giggle and a crunch,
Every nibble's quite the punch.

Layers of Delight

Torn and crisped, a stack awakes,
Savory options, oh what fakes!
Barbecue whispers, sour cream sighs,
Layers deep, twisty surprise.

Open one, and others flee,
Crispy crunch, eludes the spree.
Pick a flavor, maybe turn,
For a laugh, when snacks discern.

A Crunchy Odyssey

A voyage through flavors bold,
From cheddar dreams to spicy gold.
Each bite brings giggles galore,
With crunch so loud, you'll want more.

Chasing crumbs like secret finds,
In hidden nooks, tastebud binds.
Every crunch is quite the quest,
Join the journey, it's the best!

Savoring the Unseen

Hidden wonders in a pack,
Mystery flavors, no turn back.
Each bite holds a laugh or two,
Silly munches just for you.

Grab a chip, embrace the fun,
Count the crunches, one by one.
With every crunch, share a cheer,
Unexpected joys draw near.

Tasting the Unknown

I opened a packet, what will I find?
A flavor so strange, it's one of a kind.
With a crunch and a munch, I take a dive,
Is it sweet, is it savory? It's hard to describe!

Each bite is a chance, a roll of the dice,
A surprise in my mouth, oh, isn't it nice?
A burst of confusion, my taste buds collide,
In the world of snackland, I take a wild ride!

Mixed Crunch and Whimsy

In a bowl of snacks, who knows what's in there?
Some cheese-flavored wonders, a hint of despair.
Oh look, what's this? A chip shaped like stars!
I'll toss in some pickles, they'll fly to Mars!

With laughter and giggles, I share with my crew,
These odd little munchies keep us in a chew.
Is it pickle, or fudge? What have I got?
In every grim bite, there's a twist and a plot!

Once Bite at a Time

Just one little nibble, I promise, it's fun!
But that chip's got a kick; oh boy, what a run!
There's a taste explosion, I'm lost in the swirl,
 Is it cheddar or chili? I give it a twirl!

With friends all around, we munch and we crunch,
Each chip we devour, is served with a punch.
Every flavor is weird, every crunch brings a laugh,
 We'll snack through the night, it's our silly craft!

The Unexpected Bag

I grabbed a small bag, for a movie delight,
But what's this surprise? A flavor that bites!
"Is this chocolate potato?" I muse with a grin,
This combo of chaos is reeling me in!

In the depths of the bag, there's a tingle and thrill,
A crunch of pure laughter, it gives quite a chill.
Each chip a new venture, a gamble we take,
In this wacky world, we're awake for the shake!

Beautifully Seasoned Moments

In a bowl of joy, we dive on in,
Crunching laughter, where to begin?
Salt and humor sprinkled around,
Every chip a treasure that we've found.

With a twist of fate, and flavors bold,
A crunchy tale that never gets old.
Salsa on the side, smiles in the air,
Moments like this, beyond compare.

The Flavor Spectrum

Barbecue bright, a smoky delight,
Cheddar explosion, igniting the night.
Sour cream giggles dance on a chip,
Every bite brings a comedic trip.

Cool ranch dreams, a wild ride awaits,
Each crunch a story, a twist of fates.
With every flavor, laughter arrives,
A taste of the zany that keeps us alive.

Each Chip a New Story

In the snack drawer, stories unfold,
Each little piece, a saga retold.
A salty crunch echoes in glee,
A bite of adventure, just wait and see.

On a picnic bench, under the sun,
Chips spill laughter, oh what fun!
Cheesy puns and onion dips,
Life is a riot with these little trips.

A Palette of Surprises

From plain to wild, flavors that pop,
In this chipsy world, we can't stop.
A zesty zing, a spicy spree,
Who knew a snack could bring such glee?

Gather your friends, let's munch and munch,
Each crispy delight, a joyous munch crunch.
Jokes and crumbles scattered like bits,
In every flavor, humor sits.

The Taste of the Unknown

In a world of flavors, twist and shout,
You never know what you'll find out.
One day it's cheesy, the next is hot,
Surprises hidden, oh what a lot!

Each chip a challenge, each crunch a game,
Some are quite tame, others bring fame.
With every bite, a giggle escapes,
As the flavors dance and hilarity reshapes.

Crunchy Anticipations

Peeking in bags with eager eyes,
What flavor awaits, what tasty surprise?
Will it be spicy or sweet as a dream?
Crunch noises echo, laughter starts to beam.

Every chew sings, a chorus of fun,
Even when bites don't go as we'd run.
A little too salty? Well, that's okay!
Just grab another bag and dance away!

Salted Twists and Turns

Twist open the bag, a world to explore,
Each chip a ticket to what's in store.
Sour, sweet, or just plain bizarre,
Each crunchy crunch takes you quite far.

With flavors galore, who knows what will stick?
I swoon over vinegar's zippy kick.
Fried to perfection or bland as can be,
Every bite leads to hilarity free!

Mysterious Morsels

Caught in a crunch, what's lurking inside?
Jalapeño jigs or a ranch-flavored ride?
A bite of surprise, oh what a jest,
In this crispy world, we're truly blessed.

So open that bag, let the fun begin,
Each chip is a story, a flavorful win.
Munch and giggle, share with a friend,
In this crunchy adventure, the laughter won't end!

A Symphony of Snacks

In the pantry, treasures hide,
A crunch, a munch, a joyful ride.
Flavors dance like a raucous band,
With every bite, a taste so grand.

Chips that crackle, like laughter's call,
Sour, sweet, we savor all.
A picnic feast of odd delight,
When hunger strikes, we take a bite.

The Sweet and Savory Journey

Crispy treats in a paper sack,
Twists and turns, there's no turning back.
Caramel hugs a salty kiss,
Every nibble brings pure bliss.

Pickles and chocolate, quite the pair,
A quirky combo, beyond compare.
Taste buds tango, so bold and bright,
With every crunch, we grin in delight.

Bits of Surprise

Open the bag, oh what a sight,
Colors pop, flavors ignite.
Will it be cheesy, or ranchy cheer?
A mystery snack, oh dear, oh dear!

Each bite's a gamble, a silly game,
Crunchy reasons to stake your claim.
A burst of flavor, a giggling spree,
Snacktime's a circus, wild and free.

Paths of Peculiar Flavor

Roaming through aisles, with eyes so wide,
Longing for crunch, a savory ride.
Each packet whispers its own tale,
Of spicy journeys and sweet prevail.

Unexpected tang brings a laugh,
In every bag, we find our path.
Embrace the wacky, let's all cheer,
For snacks so strange, we hold so dear.

A Flaky Expedition

In the cupboard, a surprise,
A bag that tries to hide.
Crispy whispers catch my ear,
Oh, what secrets lie inside?

I open wide with eager hands,
A puff of air escapes.
Each chip a tale of salty lands,
In my mouth, they shape and gape.

Some bring joy, some leave a crunch,
A mess I cannot ignore.
With every bite, I laugh and munch,
Adventure in each savory score.

Crumbled pieces on the floor,
The dog thinks it's a feast!
What was that flavor, I want more—
A salty vacation, at least!

Exploratory Snacking

In the pantry, treasures hide,
A treasure map of taste.
Each bag a journey, fortune bonafide,
Munching cannot go to waste.

Flavors clash, a spicy war,
Sour cream versus cheese.
In my mouth, they dance and soar—
A symphony of crunch with ease.

Shattered bits of every hue,
Colorful bits of zest.
Each taste a surprise debut,
Never knowing what is best.

A bold pickle dips his toes,
In barbecue's warm embrace.
Unlocking secrets as it goes,
A snack, a joke, a taste of grace!

Unraveling the Unexpected

Peeking within a shiny pack,
A riot of shapes awaits.
Some round, some flat, wild in their knack,
Each bite opens new gates.

A chip that crumbles with a grin,
A mystery to unravel.
What's the taste lurking within?
Gorgeously chaotic travel.

Old secrets whisper from the fats,
In a crunch, they send a cheer.
Addicted to these snacky chats,
I munch with glee and beer.

From ranch to sweet to spicy zing,
Each chip a curious friend.
In this munchy, epic fling,
To the bottom, we won't descend!

Revelations of the Crunch

Oh, the sound of crispy bliss,
A crackle as I pop!
Every chip, a salty kiss,
I know I'll never stop.

In the garden of delights,
From onion to barbecue.
It's a world of snacking sights,
A rapture to pursue.

With each crunch, laughter flows—
An orchestra of taste.
Chasing flavors, never slows,
A silly, savory race.

In the end, it's just a bag,
But what joy can ensue!
Consider me a chip-loving brag,
For surprise is always true!

Tempting Tastes Discovered

In a shiny bag I dive,
With flavors that come alive.
Barbecue or sour cream,
Which one's gonna make me beam?

I take a crunch, it's quite a ride,
Each chip's a flavor I can't abide.
Sometimes sweet, sometimes hot,
With every bite, I love my lot.

Oh, the joy of a crinkly sound,
When munching's the best thing I've found.
Just like surprises in strange skies,
I never know what meets my eyes.

Chips of Chance

A crunch in the dark, a mystery awaits,
Chips of fate on my dinner plates.
Will it be cheddar, or a wild spice?
Every handful, a roll of the dice!

I pick one that looks like a star,
Turns out the flavor's bizarre.
Like a roller coaster ride so fast,
Each chip's a blast from the unknown past.

Friends gather round with laughter loud,
As we share our chips, feeling proud.
In the mix, giggles fill the air,
Silly snacks, none can compare.

Munching on Mysteries

In the bowl, a colorful display,
Each one hides a taste like a play.
Salt and vinegar, or wasabi flair?
Guessing the crunch, give it a dare!

A crunch that tickles and makes me grin,
Some flavors draw me right in.
I munch, I laugh, I make my guesses,
Each bite leads to secretesses.

Oh, the flavors that make me dance,
A silly snack in a playful trance.
With friends beside, we dive right in,
Chowing down on this tasty win.

The Full Flavor Experience

Curiosity in every bag,
Each flavor a chance for a brag.
Ranch or chili, what should I pick?
The suspense makes my heart do a kick!

With cheesy smiles and crunchy bites,
We host our own fun snacky nights.
Every chip tells a story so bright,
In this crispy world, we take flight.

So here's to flavors that make us cheer,
In every nibble, our joys appear.
Through twists and turns, we taste and share,
A snacking adventure beyond compare.

Whispers from a Snack Bag

In the cupboard, they sit tight,
Crinkled bags, a cheerful sight.
Each flavor holds a secret treat,
A crunch awaits, oh what a feat!

Salty tales of popcorn dreams,
Cheesy whispers, or so it seems.
Barbecue banter, sweet delights,
A crunchy party on late nights!

Tortilla chips with salsa bold,
Mingle stories never told.
Every bite, a giggle loud,
Snacktime makes us feel so proud!

With every rustle, joy we find,
Unexpected laughs, so well designed.
In each crunch, a silly dance,
Join the fun, give chips a chance!

The Unwrapping

Peel the cover, what a thrill,
Foil whispers, can't keep still.
Golden treats all stacked in rows,
What's inside? The mystery grows!

Pick a flavor, any kind,
Sour, spicy, they're intertwined.
Chomping thoughts and witty bites,
A feast that sparks our silly sights!

Laughter bubbles like soda pop,
Crunches mimic a playful hop.
Each wrapper crinkles, joy released,
With every munch, we're quite the feast!

So gather round, let's share this snack,
With each unwrap, there's no lack.
Snacktime antics, fun galore,
Munch away, who could want more?

Secrets in Every Munch

Hidden treasures in every chip,
A salty wink, a playful quip.
Crunches echo, giggles arise,
In every bite, a small surprise!

Nacho cheese, a zestful cheer,
Barbecue hugs that bring us near.
Each flavor tells its own clear tale,
In this snack world, we shall prevail!

Dip them deep or sing a song,
Snacktime joy can't be wrong.
With every crunch, the fun ignites,
Let's munch loudly, to our delights!

So share your chips, don't be shy,
In this bag, we'll soar and fly.
Each lovely munch, let laughter shine,
In crunchy realms, our spirits align!

The Crunch Chronicles

Gather 'round for tales so bright,
In crinkly bags through day and night.
Oh, the legends that we'll share,
Of crunchy bites beyond compare!

Once a chip dared to flip and fall,
Told a joke, and caused a brawl.
Salsa danced, and guac was grand,
Together they made quite a band!

Doritos whispered to the fries,
Crunchy secrets, oh what a surprise.
With every crunch, we start to glide,
Through silly stories, chips as our guide!

From party platters, we'll take a stand,
Relishing flavors, oh so grand.
So take a seat, enjoy the crunch,
In this tasty tale, there's never a punch!

Flavors from the Unknown

Open a bag, what will it be?
A taste of pickle or BBQ spree?
Each crunch a gamble, a bold little bite,
Who knows if it's wrong, or just might be right?

Mystery flavors, they dance on the tongue,
Like singing cats and a fat little bug.
Chili, and ranch, all mixed in a whirl,
Eating these snacks makes my head gently twirl.

A Handful of Happy Accidents

Dropped chip on the floor, a dust bunny lands,
I pick it back up with my hungry hands.
A surprising crunch draws a giggle from me,
This snack was meant for an impromptu spree!

Unplanned delights, oh what a thrill,
Each bite an adventure, a taste never still.
Mustard and onion? Who would have guessed!
Accidentally delicious, I'm thoroughly blessed!

Crushed Dreams

A bag half empty, dreams slightly crushed,
Like my hopes of a snack that can't be hushed.
Salted and broken, a sad little heap,
Yet I munch on the remnants, oh not too deep.

Look at these crumbs, they tell a fine tale,
Of flavors forgotten, like a lonely snail.
Dip in the salsa, make it all right,
Even shattered hopes can taste quite light!

Popped Expectations

I opened a pack, excited, you see,
Expecting a burst, like sweet jubilee.
But in the first munch, what's this funky twist?
Cherry and cheese? Oh, how could I miss!

Disappointment crumbles, I'll try it once more,
Barbecue donuts? Who knew chips wore lore?
Each pop is a wonder, a twist of fate,
Crunching through chaos, it's never too late!

Flavors Unwrapped

Each wrapper a secret, a giggle, a cheer,
What wacky creation will soon disappear?
Mystic nachos or a ginger surprise,
I dive into snacks with wide-open eyes.

Potato parade, oh delightful fandango,
From spicy to sweet, I'm ready to tango.
Every crinkle and crunch, like a quirky dance,
In this wild little world, I just take a chance!

When Surprises Unfold

In a world of flavors vast,
You never know what's coming fast.
A crunch, a munch, a fleeting taste,
Some wacky bites you just can't waste.

A pickle-flavored chip shows up,
Where did it hide? In what odd cup?
You giggle at the nonsense found,
With every bite, pure joy abounds.

Some sweet and salty mix and match,
Each snacktime brings a brand-new catch.
You reach inside, what will you get?
A strange delight, no time for regret.

So grab a seat, let's dig right in,
Embrace the chaos, let the fun begin!
With every crunch, a laugh unfolds,
Through every nibble, silliness molds.

Bagged Adventures Await

Open the bag, what will you find?
A burst of flavor, how well-defined!
Some are cheesy, some are hot,
In this wild mix, forget what you thought.

Potato treasures stacked on high,
With every crunch, we reach for the sky!
Flavors tango, flavors jive,
Inside this bag, we're alive!

A surprise from the depths of the pack,
A BBQ chip gave me quite the whack!
Each bite tells tales, I never knew,
It's a comedy show with a salty view.

So fill your bowl, let the laughter soar,
With each new flavor, you'll crave for more!
Adventures in crunch, let's take a ride,
With every snack, pure joy inside!

Tasting the Twists of Fate

A swirl of spices in every bag,
You never know what'll make you brag.
A chip that crackles, a chip that snaps,
With giggles hiding in zesty wraps.

Sour cream dreams and onion sings,
Every bite brings silly flings.
Surprises wait with each little munch,
Who knew fate could be so much fun to crunch?

Eyes wide open, my snack attack,
Which flavor next? There's no looking back!
Explore the twist of every taste,
In this wild world, there's no time to waste.

So snack on dreams, in every bite,
With twists of flavor, we take flight.
Laughs and chips go hand in hand,
In this crunchy, giggly, snack-filled land!

The Crunchy Path Less Taken

On a trail of snacks, I boldly roam,
Each little chip feels like home.
Ranch dressing flavor joins the fun,
Crunching loudly, I am not yet done.

Unexpected bites, take a chance,
A spicy surprise makes me dance!
Laughter erupts with every crunch,
A gourmet ride, let's feast for lunch!

Dare to chew what others fear,
Bold new flavors that bring good cheer.
With every chip, a story spun,
In this quirky world, I'm never done!

So come join me on this wild ride,
With crunchy paths on every side.
Snack till we drop, let joy unfold,
In each humble bag, a treasure untold!

Crunch and Curiosity

In a world of flavor, oh so bright,
Every crunch reveals a new delight.
Some are spicy, some are sweet,
Each little piece a special treat.

Tangoing with textures, loud and clear,
What's that flavor, let's give a cheer!
Mysteries packed tight in every bite,
A shriek of joy on a mundane night.

Open the bag, hear the sound,
Where crispy treasures can be found.
Will it be cheesy, ranch, or plain?
The thrill of choice drives us insane.

Laughter erupts with each surprise,
Who knew snacks could mystify?
With crunchy tales to tell anew,
Each nibble whispers, 'Try me too!'

Hidden Treasures in Crunch

Beneath the surface, secrets hide,
Crackling whispers, flavors collide.
Digging deep into the pack,
There's joy awaiting, let's not lack.

On a mission for the rarest bite,
What will I find this happy night?
A zip of garlic, a zing of lime,
What a flavorful paradigm!

Every crunch a chance to cheer,
A tangy twist, a citrus sphere.
What's lurking in the mighty mix?
Unwrap the laughter, grab your fix!

Odd combinations make us grin,
Sweet with salty, where to begin?
Unearth the crunch, summon the fun,
Chasing flavors till we're done!

Revelations in a Bag

Peering inside this crinkly vault,
What's upon the edge, what's the result?
Corny jokes in every stack,
Silly giggles keep coming back.

In a sea of colors, bright and bold,
Secrets of taste waiting to unfold.
Every morsel a lesson in glee,
What's the next flavor? Just wait and see!

With each crunch, a story to weave,
On salty waves, we'll take our leave.
Fishy surprises or pickle joy,
Each bite brings us pure, crunchy ploy.

As the bag empties, laughter remains,
Crunching memories like the rains.
For in this tiny, tasty land,
Life's bizarre tastes are always grand!

Taste Twists and Turns

Around each corner, flavors await,
Each chip a twist, isn't it great?
Sour and creamy, bold or mild,
Treat your tongue, let it be wild!

Dancing flavors, never the same,
Join the party, play the game.
Will it crunch with a pop or crack?
Delicious surprises in every snack.

Tasting journeys to local shores,
Every crunch opens up new doors.
A maze of snacks in a hand-held sack,
Shall we venture, or hold back?

So take a plunge into that bag,
Giggles and crunches make your heart brag.
With each little nibble, there's more to explore,
A crunchy odyssey, who could ask for more?

Flavorful Fortunes

In the snack aisle, dreams collide,
Tangled flavors take a ride.
Salt and vinegar, a zesty fight,
Oh, the choices, what a sight!

Lurking in the bottom row,
Mystery chips put on a show.
Barbecue whispers, cheddar sings,
Crunchy treasures, oh the bling!

A dip in salsa, what a tease,
With every crunch, I aim to please.
But watch your bag, it may run dry,
Like laughter caught by a passing guy!

A surprise burst in every crunch,
Some will make you dance and punch.
Joy unfolds behind the seal,
Snack-time experiments, we feel!

Confetti of Flavors

With each handful, flavors clash,
A fiesta of crunch, a snack-time bash!
Sweet and spicy in a swirl,
Each chip brings a different twirl.

Pickles dance with creamy dips,
A mix that's full of tasty flips.
Colorful bags, a rainbow feast,
From salty bites to salsa's beast!

Who knew that snacks could be so bright?
In every crunch, delight takes flight.
A gourmet party in my hand,
Confetti colors from a snacky land!

Taco flavors join the fray,
Bringing giggles to the play.
Every crunch, a laugh to share,
As flavors mingle in the air!

A Crunchy Roadmap

A pathway paved with cheesy dreams,
Each step a flavor bursting seams.
Ranch and onion lead the way,
Guiding munchers through the fray.

Every chip a little guide,
To the crispy world, we can't hide.
Take a left at chili spice,
Or right for sweet—a tasty slice!

But beware the bag that's half-done,
It might turn into a flavor pun.
Each empty space a missed delight,
Roadmaps change with every bite!

And if we stop to share a grin,
Unexpected combos make us win.
Crunchy journeys lead us far,
Through snack-filled nights, we are the stars!

Unforeseen Palate Pleasures

A pinch of sweet, a hint of heat,
A joyful crunch that can't be beat.
Potato whispers, corn chips cheer,
Every munch brings laughter near.

What's this? Peppers in the mix?
A daring combo, bold as bricks!
A surprise flavor, what a kick,
Makes taste buds dance, go clickety-click!

Throw in some candy, mix it right,
A crazy combo, such delight!
Sour and sweet, a wacky jam,
These nibbling joys—we just can't scram!

So raise your bags, embrace the fun,
Each chip a blessing, love them all one.
In flavor chaos, joy we find,
A crunchy journey, perfectly designed!

The Crispy Journey

A crunchy step on a sunny day,
Flavors dancing in wild array.
Who knew a stroll could bring such cheer,
With every crunch, the world feels near.

A chip fell down, it rolled away,
Chasing it turned into a play.
With every morsel, laughter flies,
In this crisp world, joy never dies.

The crunch of crunchies, oh what a sound,
Each little nibble, a treasure found.
Trips to the pantry are quests, you see,
For each bag holds its own mystery.

So grab a seat, and take a bite,
The crispy journey is pure delight.
With friends around, the fun won't stop,
Our laughter echoes like a popping pop!

Flavors in the Wind

A gentle breeze brings scents so bright,
Chips are scattered, a munching delight.
Sour cream whispers, while barbecue sings,
Snack time is where true happiness springs.

With every flavor, a silly twist,
You never know what you might miss.
Sea salt tickles and cheese does peek,
Each crunch is laughter, can't help but speak.

Under the sun, a picnic laid,
Chipping away, worries do fade.
Every meal a flavor parade,
In this crunchy kingdom, we all get paid.

So grab your chips and let's unwind,
With flavors dancing in the mind.
Every bite becomes a story told,
In this world of snacks, both rich and bold.

Surprises Under the Seal

Cracking open a bag with a squeak,
What lies within? Each chip unique.
A treasure hunt in crinkly foil,
Where every bite is sure to embroil.

Sour and sweet, a curious blend,
Shapes that twist and sometimes bend.
Each handful yields a giggly shriek,
While mystery flavors peek and sneak.

The bag's been shaken, what a surprise,
Each crunch unveils its hidden guise.
With every sound, our hearts will race,
In the dance of flavors, we find our place.

So let's not savor, let's dive right in,
Crunch and munch, let the fun begin.
For the best of chips bring joy anew,
Surprises await for me and you.

Unexpected Zest

Beneath the surface, a crunch awaits,
With zest and zing, happiness creates.
Unpredictable bites that tickle the tongue,
Every handful is a song unsung.

From spicy to sweet, a swirl of flair,
Each little chip can pull you from despair.
Life's little nuggets, in flavors combine,
Unexpected zest, in a world so fine.

Popping flavors, first crisp, then bold,
Each crunchy morsel turns up the gold.
With friends beside and laughter loud,
In these tasty moments, we feel so proud.

So grab a pack, let's share the fun,
In the world of chips, we've all won.
For every chip tells a tale of delight,
In unexpected joy, our spirits ignite.

Surreal Snacks and Snapshots

In a bowl of colors so bright,
Pickle-flavored dreams take flight.
A chip that giggles, just my luck,
With every crunch, I feel the chuck.

The salsa winks, it knows the score,
A dance of taste, I want some more.
Each bite, a snapshot, flavors collide,
With every crunch, there's nowhere to hide.

Doodles of snacks get wild and free,
Potato whispers, "Come dance with me!"
In this crazy crunch festival glee,
I find my joy—just you wait and see!

So come and savor these quirky bites,
Pixie dust toppings with rainbow lights.
In a world of munching, laughs take the lead,
Snack adventures are all that we need.

Each Bite Tells a Story

A morsel chuckles with every crunch,
Caramel dreams in a savory bunch.
Once a plain chip, now a soirée,
Each bite a saga, hip-hip-hooray!

Spicy whispers dance with delight,
A potato star in the spotlight.
Each crunch a giggle, each sip a cheer,
As fables of flavor come ringing near.

The bag rustles secrets we hold dear,
Corny tales that bring a tear.
A chip takes wing on a voyage grand,
In the realm of munchies where dreams expand!

So gather round, let's share the fun,
With stories of snacks that weigh a ton.
A journey through flavors, both weird and bold,
In this crunchy narrative, joy unfolds.

A Medley of Flavors Unseen

In a treasure chest, a burst of zest,
I dive into flavors, oh what a quest!
From barbecue to dill, a symphony plays,
Each chip a verse in the dance of days.

Sweet and sour, like a joke gone wrong,
Every nom-nom tune sings a chipper song.
In mango madness and ocean salt,
This crunchy medley gives life a jolt!

A sprinkle of laughter, a dash of surprise,
As flavors twirl 'neath the snacker's skies.
Tortilla tango, a Pita parade,
In this bistro of bites, memories are made.

Partake in the revel, oh come take a bite,
With snacks on our side, we'll laugh through the night.
A carnival of flavors, together we roam,
In the oddest of snacks, we find our home.

Crunch, Munch, and Revel

With every crunch, I leap with glee,
A tasty tango of joy for me.
Potato poppers start a cheer,
As laughter echoes, loud and clear.

Chili dusted, sweet and bright,
A crunching party, what a sight!
We snack and munch, we dance around,
In a world of flavors, joy is found.

Garlic whispers secrets untold,
As zest and crispy tales unfold.
In every handful, smiles appear,
With every morsel, we cheer and jeer!

So grab a seat, join in the fun,
Snack adventures have just begun.
In this crunchy land, laughter sings,
As we crunch, munch, and revel in things!

Traces of Teriyaki

In a crinkly pack, flavors collide,
Teriyaki whispers, sweeps me aside.
Crunch there and then a sweet little spat,
Biting into dreams, oh where's my cat?

Taste buds dance, a party of fun,
Soy sauce dribbles, but who needs a bun?
Chips fly around, a sticky delight,
Oops! That's my shirt, oh what a sight!

Some are so salty, they could be tears,
While others are sweet, dispelling my fears.
A sprinkle of humor in every bite,
Teriyaki's charm ignites the night!

So grab a chip, share the cheer,
In this funny feast, I've nothing to fear.
Even the crumbs have a story to tell,
Beneath the laughter, all is quite swell.

The Hidden Spices

Under the surface, secrets await,
A dance of spices, oh isn't it great?
Each chip an enigma wrapped tight,
Unwrap and uncover, to your delight.

One might be hot, the next cool and bland,
Taste buds play tag, it's perfectly planned.
Sippin' that soda, crunchy in hand,
Oh look, a flavor—I can't understand!

I reach for a chip, expect some routine,
Pow! A waft of garlic, I'm caught in between.
Crispy confusions, they spark a grin,
Life's a riot with these snacks piled in.

So many crunches, odd flavors beguile,
A feast of mystery makes me smile.
In every handful, joy sneaks right in,
The hidden spices where fun begins.

Popping Surprises

Crackling laughter, a chip in the air,
What's in store? Oh, I do declare!
A pop of jalapeño, what a surprise,
One minute a snack, next minute—tears in my eyes!

Salted adventures, I'm ready to dive,
Tasting each crunch—what will arrive?
Bizarre mingling, there's cola and cheese,
A party in packets, a snack-happy tease!

From sweet to spicy, the flavors connect,
Each chip a puzzle, my taste-buds reflect.
Bursting with giggles, this crunch fest is wild,
Discovering bites, at heart I'm a child.

So pop in a chip, let the games start,
Each one a riddle that pulls at my heart.
With each satisfying crunch I find,
Life's surprises are always well-timed!

A Handful of What-Could-Be

With every handful, the questions unfold,
What could this flavor possibly hold?
Sour cream dreams, barbecue beams,
Unruly chip tangents burst at the seams.

The green ones are zesty, the red ones so bold,
Every munching moment, a story told.
They promise me tang and deliver such fun,
Who knew a snack could weigh a ton?

A chip of surprise always steals the show,
One tastes like pizza, another like snow!
In this crunchy saga, joy's tastefully mixed,
Each oh-so-quirky bite makes me ticked!

So gather the pack for a whimsical spree,
A handful of wonders, a treat just for me.
With laughter and flavor in every surprise,
What-could-be wonders light up my skies.

A Symphony of Snack Pack Wonders

In a crinkly pouch, a treasure lies,
Each chip a surprise, a crunch that flies.
Barbecue calls in a zesty song,
But sour cream winks, saying, "Come along!"

Doritos dance in a cheesy romance,
While pretzels play coy in a salty glance.
A medley of flavors, each bite's a cheer,
Snack time's a symphony, let's bring on the beer!

Munching and crunching, we share a laugh,
Every bite we take, a delightful gaffe.
In this tasty chaos, we're all in the zone,
Each chip that we savor, feels like home.

So when life throws snacks, grab a handful quick,
From sweet to savory, it's all just a trick!
With flavors colliding and laughter galore,
Snack packs remind us, there's always more!

Unraveled Crisps and Twists

Unraveling joy in a crispy delight,
Some chips sing loud, others whisper at night.
A twist of lime, a dance of spice,
Each munch reveals something extra nice!

The packet is crumpled, the crumbs on the floor,
Yet these crunchy treasures leave us wanting more.
With each silly crunch, comes a snickering sound,
Snack attacks happen, it's chaos unbound!

Potato parade, lettuce stay strong,
When flavors collide, there's no room for wrong.
We dig in with glee, it's a party on cue,
Each chip's a joke, and we're the punchline too!

So here's to the munchies, that crunch in the night,
With laughter and snacks, everything's right.
Bags burst with joy, and troubles unroll,
Crisps and twists tangled, that's how we roll!

The Flavor of the Unknown

Open the bag, what will we find?
A mystery blend to unwind the mind.
Honey mustard whispers a sweet little dare,
While jalapeño's zesty, catches us unaware!

Every chip an adventure, a path unexplored,
Some leave us puzzled, others adored.
With laughter and crunches, we journey along,
In this world of snacks, we all sing our song.

What's this one? A swirl of the strange?
A flavor explosion that starts to derange!
With every bite taken, new stories unfold,
Each snack a surprise, a treasure to hold.

So embrace the unknown; let's take a chance,
In the snack universe, let's do a dance.
Between savory bites, let's live in the fun,
For every chip crunched, another day won!

Snack Time Revelations

At the table of snacks, we gather 'round,
A chorus of crunching, the happiest sound.
Potato, corn, even seaweed in play,
Each revelation's a tasty buffet!

A chip spins tales of flavors unknown,
With secret ingredients, it's never alone.
Salted, sweetened, packed into bliss,
Who knew each bite could taste like a kiss?

In the land of munchies, we laugh and we share,
Building up flavors, a culinary affair.
With friends by our side and snacks on our plates,
Snack time revelations open up gates.

So let's live in the moment, grab another handful,
Each crunchy delight feels like a good pull.
In this quirky adventure, we savor the fun,
With laughter and chips, we're never outdone!

www.ingramcontent.com/pod-product-compliance
Lightning Source LLC
Chambersburg PA
CBHW051659160426
43209CB00004B/954